THE ADVENTURES OF CULCO AND CHACHO

Written by Bella Little & Patricia Garza Pinto
Illustrated by Amy Koch Johnson

This Book is Dedicated to:

Bella's beloved family ~
her mother, Monica,
her stepmother, Sarah,
her daddy, Grant
and her precious little brother, Jackson!

This Book Belongs To:

____

It Starts with Storytelling

For almost 4 years, Lita has spent almost every week at Bella's home. Bedtime is a special time of connection with childlike laughter and giggling, as Lita slips into the bottom level of Bella's trundle bed. After Mommy reads a book to Bella, turns off the light, and leaves the room, Bella says, "Lita, will you tell me a story?"

Lita began creating off the wall stories and eventually invited Bella to contribute to the storytelling. One thing led to another, and **The Adventures of Culco and Chacho** was born.

Culco, a sweet gentle donkey, and his best friend, Chacho, a wise, courageous chihuahua, were both born on a rancho in Mexico.

Culco loved sweets........

and Chacho loved the sky, earth, flowers, creeks, sun, stars, rocks, trees and all that Mother Nature provided.

The rancho had lots of animals
and plenty of space to jugar...

...along with a handful of orphans
who played with Culco and Chacho.

Culco and Chacho were very feliz to live at
Rancho Abuelas de Luz. Or…in English…
Ranch of the Grandmothers of Light.
There were four grandmothers who cooked
for the children and looked after the animals.

There was Corazon, Alma, Sabia and Amora.
The grandmothers were great cooks and
wonderful teachers to Culco, Chacho, and the
orphans.

The **rancho** had lots of pretty golden marigolds, pink dahlia flowers and plenty of prickly cactus plants. And...every day the **abuelas** cooked delicious homemade food.

The sun was bright and hot. A large and small
tumbleweed rolled in front of the water fountain,
across the ground. There was a warm gentle
breeze that blew through the long hair on Culco's
back.

Chacho rocked side to side in his sarape hammock and was almost asleep when Culco abruptly stopped nibbling on his ear of corn and yelled,

"Chacho, let's go on an adventure!"

Culco was so loud and excited, that he startled Chacho awake from his afternoon siesta and Chacho nearly fell out of his hammock. Chacho was not happy.

"Culco, you scared me awake and why are you eating again so soon?! We just had a delicious homemade breakfast of huevos rancheros with abuela's tasty fresh roasted salsa! Besides…where would we go? We've never been off the rancho. Plus, I would miss Abuela Alma's homemade tortillas," said Chacho with a smile.

"Chacho…I'm kind of bored on the rancho. Besides, the orphans are not so little, they are growing so fast and a couple of them are getting too heavy to ride on my back. Let's go someplace different!" said Culco.

"Donde? Where would we go? We've never been off the rancho!" asked Chacho.

Culco looked dismayed.

"Okay, I'll think of someplace different to go," said Chacho, as he scratched his head.

"I know! Let's go to the big fiesta next week. I heard it's very fun with pinatas filled with lots of sweet candies!" said Chacho.

"The fiesta in the pueblo? I'd like to travel and have a real adventure!" said Culco.

"Trust me, my beloved donkey friend, this fiesta will be a big adventure for us since we've never been off the rancho," said Chacho.

"Okay, it's a deal. We'll go to the fiesta in the pueblo, as long as I get lots of sweet caramelos from the colorful pinatas!" said Culco, smiling his huge donkey teeth.

While Culco and Chacho discussed their first adventure, the Abuelas were busy in the cocina making tamales, pozole and sweet bunuelos.

As the orphans got ready for bed. Culco and
Chacho decided it was time for bed too.

It was a cool, dark starry night, and all the animals were sound asleep in the granero. Culco and Chacho were in a deep sleep. Chacho growled and barked little chihuahua "bow wow" sounds, and Culco tossed and turned, while making loud donkey "hee haw" sounds as he slowly kicked the air with his hoofs. The granero was so quiet, that you could hear the twinkle of the nighttime stars in the black sky.

Then, Chacho fell out of his sarape hammock and landed on top of Culco, waking them both.

"Chacho…why did you fall on me?!" asked startled Culco.

"Perdon," said sleepy eyed Chacho. "I guess I had a sueno. It felt so real. And I was having so much fun at a fiesta!" said Chacho.

"De verdad?! No way, cuz I had the same dream…I was at a fiesta in the pueblo, said Culco.

"Wow! Well…maybe this means our hearts are finally connected since we had the same dream!" said Chacho.

On the rancho, Abuela Corazon often talked with the animals in the granero and told them,

"If humans could only open their hearts, like the animals and love unconditionally…they would be more connected with each other, and share the same dreams. Remember…humans can only do this when they connect with the pure love in their hearts."

And because Culco and Chacho loved each other unconditionally; they could connect hearts and share the same dreams. Culco and Chacho were now wide awake and so happy that they shared the fiesta dream. They went outside under the bright luna and estrellas and danced.

Because Culco and Chacho never before left the rancho, caminando to the fiesta in town was a grand aventura, and they saw things they never saw before. Culco and Chacho walked past a small, very beautiful iglesia with a large bell tower that rang loud pretty tones.

Horchata
Helado

A man on the corner stood near a push cart and was selling cold helado and tasty beverages. The vendor wore dusty old huaraches and an old straw hat. He had a thick black mustache and a couple of missing teeth with a big beautiful smile!

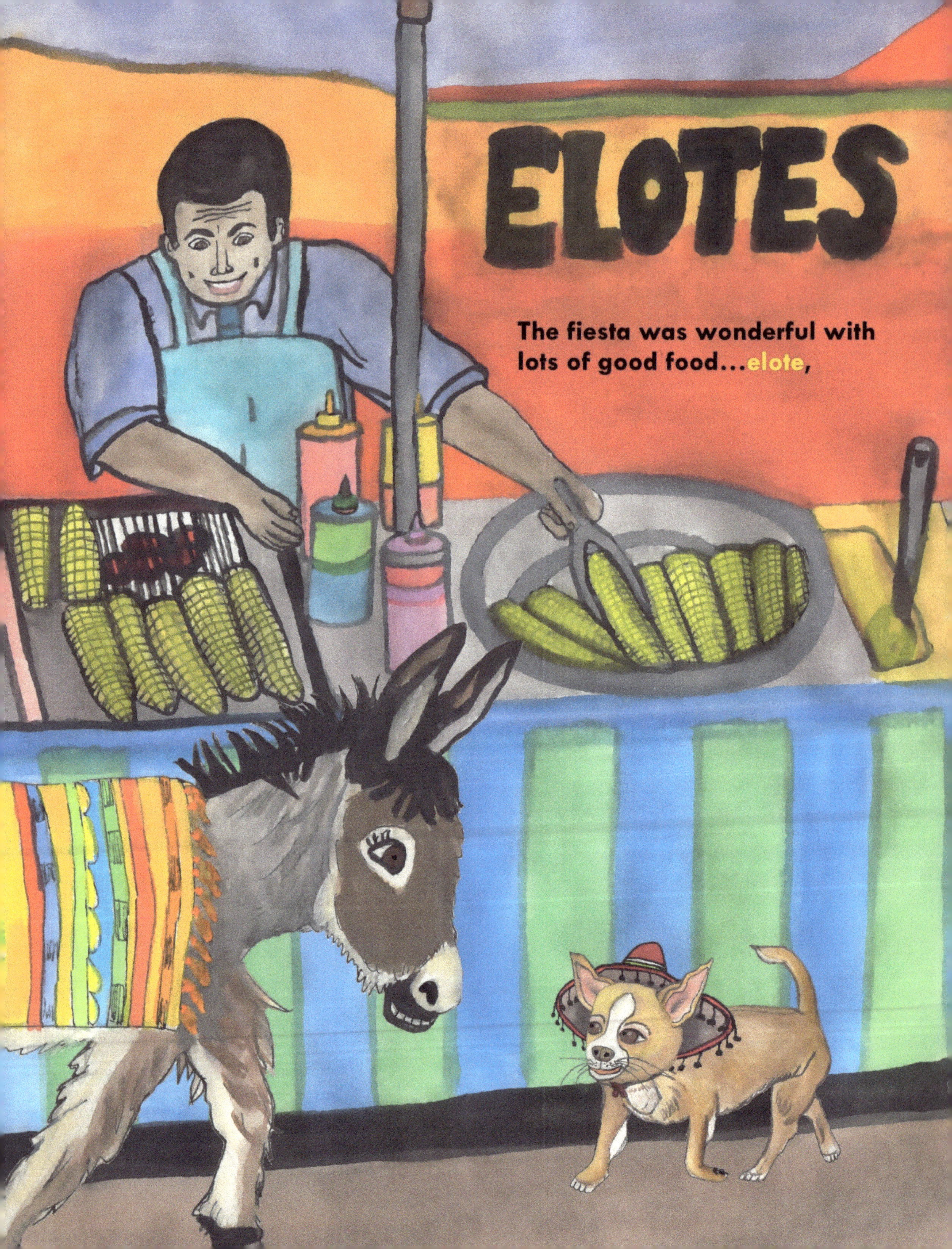

ELOTES
The fiesta was wonderful with lots of good food…elote,

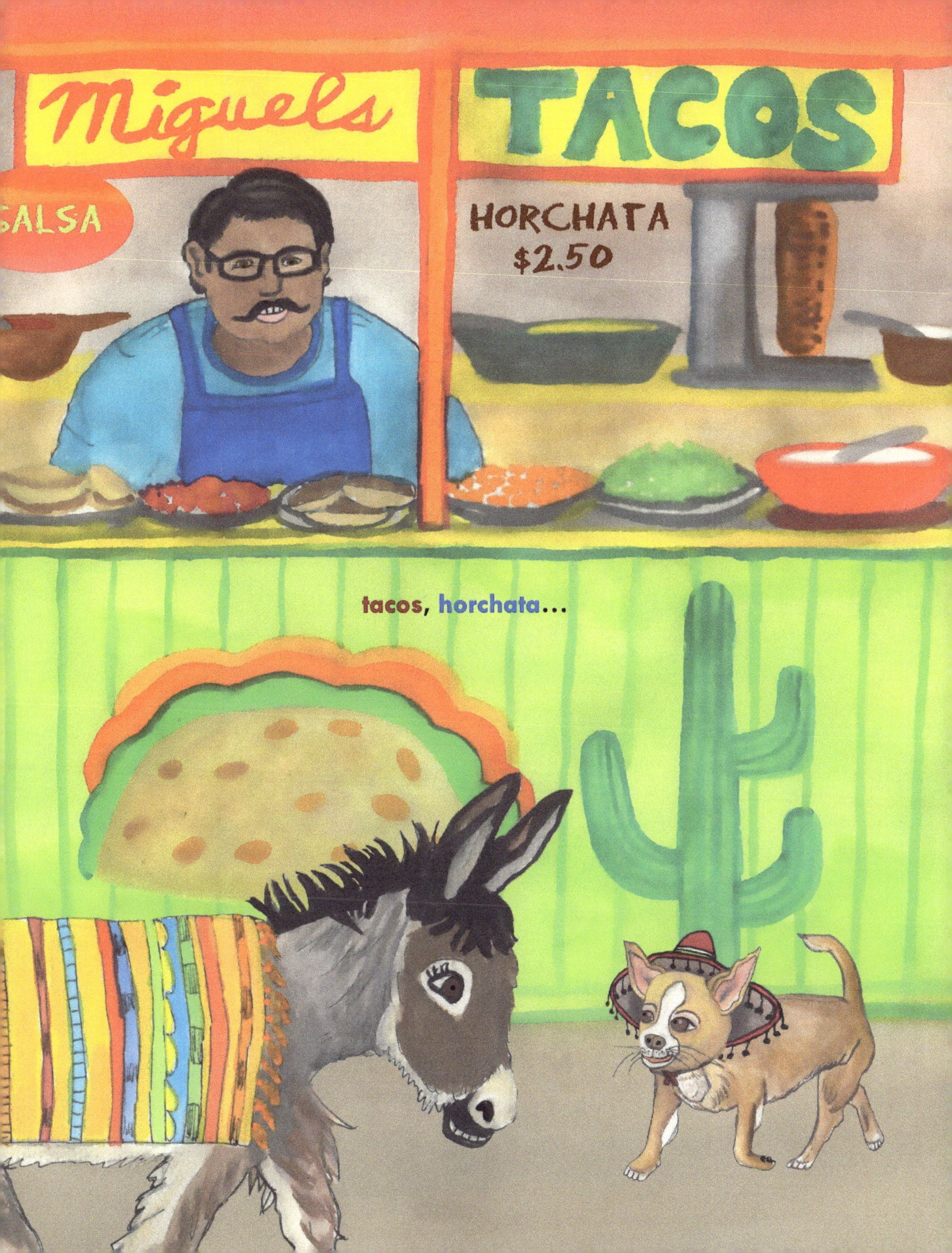

tacos, horchata…

And mariachi musicians who played large guitars, dancing, laughing and many candy filled piñatas on every corner of the plaza.

Culco and Chacho ate tacos, danced, laughed and enjoyed some dulce from the pinata, which had fallen on the ground when the blindfolded children cracked it open.
Piñatas
Cotton Can

And, since they had never before left the rancho, they were very happy to have this new adventure.
CANDY APPLES

Culco and Chacho were so tired from the long day traveling to and from the fiesta and having so much fun while at the fiesta, that they slept in late…

And then awoke to a warm sunny dia, and a full day of rancho chores. While doing their chores, they were unusually quiet, because they were both daydreaming about their next exciting adventure. And...You can bet their next adventure will be even more exitante. You will just have to wait and see.

The End...for now!

WORD TRANSLATION & PRONUNCIATION

rancho – ranch / ran-cho 

jugar – play / who-gar 

feliz – happy / feh-leez 

Rancho Abuelas de Luz – Grandmothers of Light Ranch /  ran-cho-ah-bwe-lahz-day-looz

abuelas – grandmothers / aub-wel-ahs 

siesta – nap / see-es-tah 

huevos rancheros – ranch eggs / way-vows-raan-cheh-ros

salsa – a variety of Mexican sauces / saal-suh 

tortilla – thin flat pancake / tore-tee-ah 

donde – where / don-day

fiesta – party / fee-es-tah 

piñatas – hollow paper mâché characters or animals filled with candy / peen-yah-tas 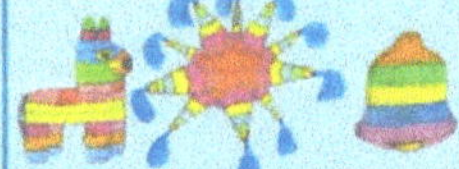

pueblo – town / poo-eb-low

caramelo – candy / cah-rah-mel-o 

cocina – kitchen / ko-si-na 

tamales – seasoned meat wrapped in corn meal dough and steamed or baked / tah-mah-lez

pozole – traditional soup made with pork or chicken / 
poe-zoe-lay
bunuelos – sweet, thin, round fried pastry sprinkled with
cinnamon and sugar / boon-wel-los 

granero – barn / grah-neh-roe 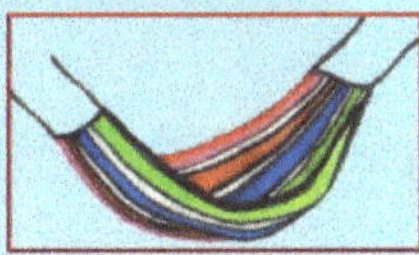

sarape – shawl / sah-rop-ay

perdon – sorry / pear-done

sueno – dream / suane-yo

De verdad – really / de-ver-daud

corazon – heart / cor-ah-zone

luna – moon / loo-na 

estrellas – stars / e-stray-aus 

caminando – walking / cah-mee-non-doe 

aventura – adventure / ah-ven-too-ra

iglesia – church / ee-glay-seea 

helado – ice cream / e-lah-doe 

huaraches – sandals / hwah-rah-chays 

elote – corn on the cob / e-lo-tay 

tacos - a traditional Mexican dish consisting of a small hand-
sized corn or wheat tortilla topped with a filling /
taa-kowz

horchata – milky drink made from ground almonds or rice / or-chah-ta 

mariachi - a small, strolling, Mexican band consisting usually of trumpeters, guitarists, and violinists / mar-e-yah-chee

dulce – sweet; sugary treat / dool-seh

dia – day / dee-ah

excitante – exciting / ex-ci-ton-tay

WORD TRANSLATION FOR NAMES OF THE GRANDMOTHERS

Corazon – Heart / cor-ah-zone

Alma – Soul / all-mah

Sabia – Wise / sah-bee-ah

Amora – Love / ah-mor-ah

About the Authors

"My Relationship with Bella?" Lita's eyes well up. "The word that comes to mind is endearing. Without a shadow of doubt, I would take a bullet for her. Bella is the apple of my eye, the love of my life. She's my soul, the gift that taught me how to tap into my inner child and know that I am more than a warrior woman, that I am also a precious white light inner child. Through our storytellings and book writing, my inner child has awakened and opened and remembered how to show herself, how to live for joy and laughter, and to know that beautiful healing comes from that. Through Bella, much generational healing is taking place that is deeper than meets the eye."

Bella is a young artist, pitcher, and Girl Scout, with a love for softball, her two dogs, Ruby and Oliver, her family, and her friends. Like Culco and Chacho, she has no boundaries around what family is or isn't and cherishes her stepmother and half-brother as deeply as her mother and father. Bella was 9 years old when she created this book with her Lita. She lives in Southern California.

Lita, aka Patricia Garza Pinto, is a holistic wellness practitioner offering energy medicine healing for women who suffer chronic emotional and physical pain...uplifting and supporting "sisters" who do not yet have the emotional, mental, physical, or spiritual wherewithal to face the trauma and experiences that have kept them stuck in life. Experiencing the personal traumas in her first decades of life equipped Patricia with the ability to tap into her inner warrior woman, rise up from victimhood, and fulfill her purpose of guiding women to face their wounds and trauma, feel, cry, dig deep and alchemize the pain and the learning, and leave the wounds behind, to create a strong body, mind and spirit, internally and externally. As above, so below.

Lita, aka Patricia, lives on the mountains of Idyllwild, California. For more information on Patricia's services, including women's retreats, visit Divinemountainretreat.com

The End
for now.........